P9-AZV-178

Me, Myself, and God

DAVID ALLEN SORENSEN

Augsburg • Minneapolis

For
Jan and Jay,
brothers, friends, cuffies

ME, MYSELF, AND GOD
A Young Christian Book for Boys

Scripture quotations unless otherwise noted are from the Holy Bible: New International Version. Copyright 1978 by the New York International Bible Society. Used by permission of Zondervan Bible Publishers.

Scripture quotations marked TEV are from The Good News Bible, Today's English Version, copyright 1966, 1971, 1976 by American Bible Society. Used by permission.

Photos: Jim Cronk, 8; Renaud Thomas, 18; Richard West, 26, 58; CLEO Freelance Photo, 36; James L. Shaffer, 78.

Library of Congress Cataloging-in-Publication Data

Sorensen, David Allen, 1953–
    Me, myself, and God : a young Christian book for boys / David Allen Sorensen.
        p. cm.
        Summary: A collection of stories about boys who learn that God loves them just the way they are.
        ISBN 0-8066-2442-6
        1. Children's stories, American.   [1. Christian life—Fiction.
    2. Short stories.]   I. Title.
    PZ7.S718Me   1990
    [Fic]—dc20   89-49096
                                                           CIP
                                                            AC

The paper used in this publication meets the minimum requirements of American National Standard for Information Sciences—Permanence of Paper for Printed Library Materials, ANSI Z329.48-1984.   ∞™

Manufactured in the U.S.A.   AF 9-2442
94   93   92   91   90   1   2   3   4   5   6   7   8   9   10

Contents

About This Book

Wouldn't it be fun to be invisible so we could listen in on what people really think of us? I've daydreamed about that since I was a kid. I've been thinking, though: Maybe it would be fun, but maybe it would just hurt our feelings.

This book won't make you invisible, but it will let you peek in on some characters who are something like you, going through lives that are normal one moment and amazing the next. They will show you something about themselves that will really make you think. You will see yourself in many stories. You will meet:

- Andy, the "zero," the guy they say is "lower than a geek";
- "Tree," the tall, street fighter who would rather stay in the basement;
- Sammy, the guy whose mouth is going to get him in big trouble;

- Mary Anne, beautiful, "perfect"—with a perfectly awful secret;
- Walter, the boy who defused a nuclear bomb and may one day be a pastor;
- The Amazing Eddie, and his more-than-amazing neighbor;
- Spencer, the kid who practically invented the "wide-eyed, innocent-puppy look" that he's sure the girls go for; and
- Nate, the boy in black who hasn't been the same since—

Ah, but that would be telling. And I'd rather let you read the whole story, indeed, all of the stories.

Me, Myself, and God is about you, yourself, and God. You are terribly interesting—Did you know that?—because you were made by a God who is wonderfully interesting. There is a whole lifetime of things to learn about yourself and about God—and then some. You've got an eternity to learn, but let's start now.

It has been fun for me to watch and learn more about young Christians and then to weave what I have learned into these stories, stories about who you are, how you change, what you'll become. The more I learn about you and the more I learn about God, the more sure I am that you and God are the ultimate team. Together you will live an exciting life, a creative life, a life full of explorations.

Explore now with me. Let's go into each other's hearts as we share this book together. And as you

About This Book

read with the help of the Holy Spirit, you will be
touched by the heart of God.

Blessings, my friend,
David Allen Sorensen

"I pray that out of his glorious riches he may
strengthen you with power through his Spirit in
your inner being."
—Ephesians 3:16

•

*"Why can't you just look big like a basketball
player instead of act big like a high school street
fighter? You're only in seventh grade, for Pete's
sake."*
—Tree's mother

Shiner

"You've been in a fight again," Mrs. Maslow
tossed at her 13-year-old son at the beginning of a
pasta supper.

"Did you just notice?" he replied sourly, biting
into a piece of garlic toast. "I mean, I've been home
an hour with an eye that's almost swollen shut."

"You've been in your room," she replied. "Tree,
when are you going to quit fighting?"

Grandpa Joe kept his head down, concentrating
on his noodles.

"I don't pick the fights, Ma," Tree replied. "I'm
just big, so everyone assumes I want to."

"You look too tough for your own good, Tree.
Why can't you just look big like a basketball player

instead of act big like a high school street fighter? You're only in seventh grade, for Pete's sake."

Tree shoved his chair away from the table and stared at his shoes as he felt the heat of anger flush his face. His shoelaces dangled limply in every direction. Tree prided himself on the fact that he had never touched the laces of these particular shoes with his hands. They were never tied. They never would be. One day the laces would fall out and he wouldn't care.

It was important to Tree not to care about how he looked. Most of his friends were that way, too, though Tree couldn't remember anyone actually talking about it. So he worked hard to look like he didn't care how he looked. He worked so hard at it that sometimes it bothered him that he thought so much about how he looked. He caught himself looking in all the windows and mirrors he passed at the mall just to see himself flop and flow along in his old, limp clothes.

"The way I look is my business!" he said emphatically. Then he looked up to see what effect his bold words had. His mother had her eyes on Grandpa Joe as if she were asking him to support what she said. He never did. He still toyed with his noodles.

"How about trying some new blue jeans—I'll buy," she said. "And a new jean jacket with snaps that work, and maybe you can comb your hair or tie your shoes?"

Tree had heard it all before. This was the place in the argument where he always sat in moody silence.

She placed her hands on her lap. "This boy's going to be—"

"Just fine," Grandpa Joe said with quiet confidence.

Tree and his mother glanced at him quickly, then at each other. Tree shrugged. Grandpa *never* got involved in these arguments.

"He's going to be just fine," Grandpa Joe said. "Pass the parmesan cheese, please. Then give the kid some ice for his shiner."

"It won't do any good, Dad," Mrs. Maslow said. "He should have had ice on it right after it happened."

"Then get me some ice for my water and let's quit talking about what a hoodlum Tree is going to be when he grows up, Marsha," Grandpa said. "He's going to be just fine."

Grandpa Joe, sensing the surprise of his daughter and grandson at his unexpected words, looked up from his noodles and winked at Tree. At that moment, Tree felt a kind of pleasure he had never felt before.

After supper, he spent the evening as he spent six out of seven spring evenings, fine tuning and polishing ten-speed bicycles in the basement. The rest of the year, as much as he could, he spent his evenings out with his friends.

Tree worked on his own bicycles off and on almost all year long—more than was necessary—but in the spring he worked on the bikes of a couple dozen regular customers. It wasn't just the money; Tree simply felt like he did lots of things so-so in life, but he knew he was very special when he got near a good bike.

People were always surprised to find that Tree had been in business fixing bicycles for over four years, almost as long as he had been riding them. His dad had been living at home at the beginning. He told Tree he had a knack for things mechanical. Tree remembered that moment often. But his steady customers would say even more. They would say that Tree could make the bikes look like new, that the bikes whirred with precision after he had finished the spring tune-up. They would say that Tree was better than the guys in the shop on 4th Street. And so, when he would charge a little less than his competition, almost every customer would make sure he got a good tip, as well.

Tree turned the screwdriver a quarter turn more in the gearing mechanism, then flipped the lever again as he cranked the peddles on the inverted bike. Satisfied with the result, he braked the wheel, released the bike from the homemade bike stand, righted the bike, then propped it next to four others.

"You do good work," Grandpa Joe said from the stairs.

"Thanks," Tree replied quickly without looking. Then after thinking for a moment, he said, "How would you know, Grandpa? You don't know anything about fixing bicycles."

"No, but I know about milking cows," Grandpa Joe replied.

Tree smiled. He knew Grandpa liked to say some off-the-wall things now and then. "But a cow doesn't have gears," Tree said.

"So? A bike doesn't have udders."

"Oh, yeah? A cow doesn't have wheels."

"And a bike doesn't kick."

Tree's and Grandpa Joe's smiles turned into laughter.

"So why bring up the cows, Grandpa?" Tree asked. "I don't get it."

Grandpa sat low on a wooden footstool. Tree sat on the floor and leaned back against the workbench.

"Before you were born I worked as a hand at a big milking spread halfway to the big city," Grandpa said. "Worked for a fellow named Searing. There were more milk cows in his barn than in any other in the county. Searing was the best. His cows were the cleanest, they gave the most milk, his equipment was the best maintained, and his milk was top quality. Everybody knew it. But nobody could figure out why he was the best for so many years in a row. Especially since Searing didn't look like a successful, rich man; he looked like a slob."

Tree quit smiling and looked at his shoes for the second time that evening. He could guess where Grandpa was going with the story.

"Well, I asked him one day why his dairy business was so blamed good, and you know what he said?"

Tree shook his head.

"This guy Searing said it was because he made sure all the stainless steel equipment in that long barn shined. That's it."

"I don't get it," Tree answered.

"I didn't get it either," Grandpa said, "until I visited another dairy farm one day. It was dark and smudgy, all the cows were matted and dirty, and the place stunk. The people who worked in there didn't smile, and the cows acted different from Searing's cows. I can't explain it."

"Sounds like Searing was quite a guy," Tree said.

"Yup. Saw him again a couple years ago. He still wears the same unpolished boots—or a pair just as ugly, if that's possible—and he's about thirty more pounds overweight, and he still hasn't learned how to shave. But when I see him now I don't hardly even notice that stuff. I look at him and I see gleaming milk tanks and hosed-down, fresh-painted floors. And I see happy cows."

"Oh," Tree said.

Grandpa Joe stood and looked like he was getting ready to head back upstairs. Then he said, "Know what I see when I look at you, Tree?"

"I think my mom sees a mess," Tree said from the floor.

"I'm not so sure about that, but I'm not your mom, am I, boy?"

"No, sir."

"Know what I see?"

"No."

"I see a well-greased and oiled hummer of a bicycle with paint touched up and polished like new. I see people having fun on those bicycles, grateful to you

14

for doing such a good job. I see someone who makes my heart glad, Tree. That's what I see."

Tree was surprised to feel heavy tears forming in the outside corners of his eyes. He said nothing.

"I know you heard me, but you're too stubborn to say so. I haven't told you near often enough. I'm proud of you, boy," Grandpa Joe added. "Who a person is on the inside is a whole lot more important than what a person looks like on the outside, know what I mean?"

"Thanks, Grandpa," Tree said simply.

Grandpa Joe turned and thumped up the steps. From the landing at the top Tree heard him say, "Tree, know what you should do next time some other kid thinks you look like a thug and wants to pick a fight with you?"

"No, what?"

"Offer to shine up his bicycle."

"That'd sure show him, huh, Grandpa."

"You bet. Try it. It'd show him who you *really* are."

Grandpa shut the door at the top of the stairs.

Tree got up and, without thinking, began to put away his many tools, each in its place. Soon, his grandpa opened the door again just enough to shout down, "And if you want to please your old grandpa tonight, look in the family Bible where I marked it, Ephesians 3:16. It talks about what I want for you on the inside."

"Good night, Grandpa," Tree said.

Tree stopped and surveyed his tidy workshop with the shiny bikes. And he smiled. And he thought, *Grandpa sees the real me.*

Tree felt a rare kind of pleasure for the second time that evening.

Tree's prayer: Dear Lord Jesus, I guess I know how much you love me. Everyone says it's true. And I know that you know me better than anyone, even better than Grandpa Joe. Well, if the one who knows me best loves me most, then it makes me feel just . . . just . . . I don't know, relieved, I guess. Thank you for knowing me and loving me like you do. Amen.

Action idea: It's hard for people to know what someone is like on the inside. But it's easy for God to know. God made us, after all. Ask God in prayer to show you three good things about your inner self that are hard for other people to see. (Do you try especially hard in some area of your life? Are you kind to someone who isn't easy to be with? Have you ever done a good thing that almost nobody knows about?) Having trouble thinking of something? Realize that you were created in the image of God, and that in itself is an incredible thing for which you can thank God!

"How great is the love the Father has lavished on us, that we should be called children of God! And that is what we are!"
—1 John 3:1

●

"God has reserved a special set of personality traits and attitudes and gifts just for a guy named Eddie. And now you and I know what it is that makes you special; you are a child of God."
—Ishmael

The Amazing Eddie

Everybody who lived on Eddie's street knew at least two things for sure: (1) they lived on *Eddie's* street, and (2) Eddie was *amazing*. They knew these two things because Eddie told them so. He told this to each and every one of them on the day they moved into the neighborhood, and he reminded them at least once a week thereafter.

For instance, Eddie once blocked off the cul de sac—that's a fancy way to say a short, dead-end street—and would only let cars pass by if they bought lemonade from him. It wouldn't have been so bad if it had been a hot, summer day. But it was winter! People just shook their heads and muttered, "That kid's amazing!"

The Amazing Eddie

Then there was the time when Eddie made the rounds on a Saturday morning ringing doorbells and saying, "How about you let The Amazing Eddie wash the windows on your car?" It seems some vandal had gone through the neighborhood during the night slinging mud at all the windows of every car in sight.

"Young man, this is extortion," old Mrs. Whipley in the yellow house complained.

"Mrs. Whipley," Eddie replied, "I don't know what that means, but if you let me, The Amazing Eddie, wash your windows for a dollar, I'll throw in an amazing trick for nothing."

Mrs. Whipley looked perplexed. "You'll what?" she asked.

"I, The Amazing Eddie, will stand on one hand for a full minute—while using my other hand to eat three cookies and drink a glass of milk." Then he added, "You've got three cookies, don't you?"

"Will peanut butter cookies do?"

"Perfectly. You get the cookies while I wash your windshield."

Such was Eddie's control over people in the neighborhood that Mrs. Whipley promptly got three peanut butter cookies and a nice glass of milk. Eddie was polishing up the last window when she arrived.

"The dollar?" he asked.

"I wasn't born yesterday," Mrs. Whipley replied—she was fond of saying that—"You've got to do the trick first."

"That's easy," he said, taking the snack.

Then he crouched down and stepped onto his left hand. "There," he explained, "I'm standing on one hand." And he proceeded to enjoy the milk and cookies.

"Why, you're not upside down at all!" Mrs. Whipley scoffed. "You're just—"

"Standing on one hand. You owe me one dollar," he said with his mouth full.

●

The next day the Newtons pulled into the driveway of their new home in a large rented truck an hour before school let out, so The Amazing Eddie wasn't able to be there right away to tell them it was his neighborhood.

Sara Newton was hauling boxes out of the back of the truck as Eddie swept past her on his bike and skidded to a sideways stop in the loose dirt of the driveway. She jolted and almost stumbled with a box marked "fragile."

To Eddie's surprise, she recovered quickly, smiled widely, and said, "Bless you."

"Why? I didn't sneeze," Eddie countered suspiciously.

"No, I mean bless you for being the first person to welcome us to the neighborhood."

"How do you know I'm here to welcome you?" Eddie asked.

"Aren't you?"

"Yah, uh, sure, I guess I am."

20

"Well, then, come in and meet Ishmael," she said. She pushed past him and hefted her box through the door, leaving Eddie to follow slowly.

Inside, Eddie started to follow the dark-haired, dark-eyed lady into the kitchen when he almost ran into a large man in a wheelchair coming out. The man wore athletic shorts, and had no legs.

Eddie was startled. He had known people on crutches after a skiing accident, but he had never known anyone who spent most of their waking hours in a wheelchair. Not knowing what to say, he said, "I'm The Amazing Eddie."

"And I'm Ishmael Newton," the man replied. "My father was from Boston and my mother was from Egypt."

Eddie noticed that his arms, chest and shoulders were very dark and muscular under the striped summer shirt.

The man asked, "What do you get when you try to send a dead skunk in a package to your cousin in California?"

Eddie frowned, "But I don't have a cousin in—"

"You get ISH-mail," the man said and burst out laughing. "Get it? That's how you say my name."

Eddie didn't know what to say—again.

After a few moments Eddie figured out that he was not laughing at him, so he joined in the laugh.

"What makes you say you're so amazing, Eddie?"

"Because everybody says I'm amazing," Eddie answered.

"No," the man said abruptly. "You *are* amazing, but that's not why."

Eddie could tell somehow the man was testing him in a friendly way to see what he was like. He liked the feeling of having someone he didn't know pay such close attention to him.

"I'm amazing 'cause I can do tricks and things like juggling, holding my breath for almost three minutes, and naming the state capitols in alphabetical order," Eddie said proudly. But he wondered which of his best tricks he could do indoors if the man asked for a demonstration.

"Wrong again!"

"But . . . but how do you know?" Eddie could tell that the man knew something he wanted Eddie to discover and it made Eddie both excited and frustrated.

"Because I knew you were amazing the moment you walked into this house!"

"You did?"

"Absolutely. Anyway, think about it. There's a reason why you are amazing, but you haven't told me yet what it is."

Eddie had a quizzical half-grin on his freckled face.

"What other tricks can you do, Eddie?"

"I can walk on my hands," Eddie said. "See?" And he squatted down, stepped on both hands, and began to duck-walk around the dining room.

"Amazing!" Ishmael said. "But there's something else even more amazing about you. You'll see."

Eddie felt challenged. "No, you'll see," he said. "Stop on over to my backyard—the gold house over there—in ten minutes and I'll show you one of my best tricks."

"Ten minutes. You got it."

●

Eddie raced home and changed into his swim-suit. Then he pulled from the garage two long pieces of wood fitted on the ends with downhill ski mountings.

He sat on the edge of his above-ground pool in the backyard, put on a pair of low-cut boots and snapped them to the bindings on the wooden stilts.

Eddie slowly stood up in the pool and found his balance. The modified stilts and most of the boots were under water. He walked to the middle of the pool and waited. A person looking at him from the side would swear that he was walking on water!

A minute later, someone strolled around the corner of the house. It took Eddie a couple of moments to realize that the tall man walking toward him was none other than Ishmael.

"You've got legs!" Eddie cried out. In his surprise, he took a step backwards, swayed over the water first one way and then another, then splashed to his rear.

Ishmael realized that Eddie was having trouble keeping his head above water while still wearing the homemade stilts, so he ran around the pool and held him by the armpits while Eddie released himself from the bindings.

"You've got legs," Eddie sputtered once again as Ishmael helped him out of the pool.

"By golly," Ishmael replied, looking down in mock surprise. "I think you're right. Two of them. Now where did they come from? Actually, Eddie, I usually wear these things; I've just been having some trouble with sores on the stumps, so it's been good to be in the chair for a while." He helped Eddie out of the pool.

"I'm going to get out of the amazing business," Eddie said, almost meaning it. "You're the most amazing guy on the street now."

"No, Eddie," Ishmael said kindly. "You're still The Amazing Eddie. Have you figured out why?"

"Because I can walk on water—almost?"

"You're not amazing because people think you are. You're not even amazing because you can do such amazing tricks. You're amazing—listen to this—because *God has made you absolutely unique.* You're amazing because God has made you amazingly well, and God's put a real spark in you that I especially like."

"That's it?"

"That's plenty, Eddie. God has reserved a special set of personality traits and attitudes and gifts just for a guy named Eddie. And now you and I know what it is that makes you special; you are a child of God."

24

The Amazing Eddie

Eddie felt a sudden warmth from the sun, but he felt another special warmth as well as he stood before this man who seemed so powerful and yet so kind.

"You know what, Eddie?" Ishmael asked. "You don't have to do one trick or anything else to make me like you better than I do already. In fact, I still have a week before I start my new job in this new town, so I'd like to spend some time this afternoon getting to know you. That's my way of saying thanks for coming over to be the first one to welcome us."

Eddie felt as giddy as if the man had dropped in on supper and offered to eat his creamed spinach for him.

Amazing!

The Amazing Eddie's prayer: Sometimes I think I act too stupid with people, always having to be "amazing." Thank you for the new guy on the street, Ishmael. For some reason, I feel special just being around him, (and I don't even have to try so hard). Amen.

Action idea: Is there someone you like to impress because you want that person to like you? After reading about The Amazing Eddie, do you think that person might actually like you just the way you are? Is there someone who likes to try to impress you to get you to like them? Be like Ishmael with them and tell them they're already special and don't have to keep trying to prove it.

"So God created human beings, making them to
be like himself. He created them male and
female."
—Genesis 1:27 TEV

•

*"How did you know that about me?
I haven't told anybody."*
—Nate

Nate's Secret

Paul, Stella, and Joshua ran toward the pool and
jumped together into the deep end making the big-
gest cannonball *ka-thum-plash* sound anyone had ever
heard. Still, they did not succeed at getting Nate
wet. They didn't even make him flinch or say anything at all. And while the rest of the kids cheered
and laughed, Nate didn't even smile.

Stella hoisted herself from the pool and turned and
thanked the boys for helping her. Then she dripped
her way toward Nate, straightening her swimsuit and
wringing out her hair as she went.

"Hey, Nate, you're not having any fun," she called
out. Stella had known Nate since kindergarten and
had been in the same pack of friends almost from
the beginning.

"Can't a guy sit and rest?" he responded.

"Rest from what? You haven't done anything with anybody for weeks. What's wrong?"

Just because Stella wanted him to move, Nate refused to do so.

"Leave me alone, Stella," he said somberly.

"What is it? Family problems? You taking drugs? Why are you so different since school let out? I know it's none of my business, but we're all going to be in *junior high* next month, and that should be reason to celebrate!"

"Yea, whoopie doopie," he said in a low voice while twirling his index finger. "Now go away."

"Suit yourself, Skinny," she said, taking a swipe at his bony leg with her foot. "We can have fun without you." Stella couldn't see the hurt look in his eyes when she called him Skinny; his sunglasses hid his emotions too well. But she sensed that Nate tightened his body—Was it in anger?—more at the name than at the kick. The rest of the afternoon she couldn't shake the feeling that Nate was watching her very closely from under the dark glasses.

Stella thought a lot about Nate that night. She always thought more clearly at night and wondered if it had anything to do with the fact that her name meant "star." Stella thought back to the last ten times she had been with him: twice at the city pool, five days in a row at their last vacation Bible school, and three times she had just seen him walking along the road by the mall. There was something different about him during those ten encounters than in all the other years she had known him. But what was it?

Stella did what she always did when she wanted to understand something that was hard to understand. She decided to write in her journal, something she had learned from her big sister who had learned it one weekend at some retreat center.

She reached into the lefthand drawer beneath her bedroom bookcase to pull out a yellow hardcover book. She sat at her desk, sighed once, opened the book, and wrote:

"I'm supposed to just start writing without thinking too hard about what I'm writing. If I do this right I am supposed to discover things that are going on inside me that maybe I didn't even know about. So I'm doing that and tonight nothing is happening. Why? Because I can't get my mind off of Natty."

Funny, she thought, *I haven't called Nate Natty in years.*

She continued writing: "He's always been sort of a good friend, I guess. We have more in common than most of the other kids I hang around with. In fact, a few times we have shared something very special and secret. . . ."

What am I saying? she wondered. *I have a secret relationship with Nate? Why didn't I ever tell myself this before?*

She wrote, ". . . like the time when we chose the same closet for a hiding place during games at Liz's birthday party. We were on top of boxes in the back of a coat closet, so even though people looked in the closet several times they couldn't see our feet sticking out on the bottom and didn't think we were in there. We were shoulder to shoulder for what must have been an hour, and neither of us wanted to break that secret feeling that was between us."

My goodness, what if he feels the same way about our secret that I do?

"But Nate has not been the same since school let out for the summer. Why? Why? Why? Why? Just write and let it come out, self. Because, because, because, because he has been dressing in those ugly, dark, winter clothes too much. No, that's wrong. Because, because he has a disease and he's going to die before the summer is over. I hope not! Because, because, wait a second, he *is* wearing too many dark, winter clothes, and it's *summer time.* Why? Maybe I'm onto something here. Think. He is wearing all those heavy, dark clothes . . . because he is hiding something underneath. Yes! He's hiding himself . . . because he *doesn't like how he looks!*"

●

The next morning, Stella had her hair done at a beauty shop in preparation for going to her cousin's wedding that afternoon. It was a perm, the kind that looks really good when a person is all dressed up— if it turns out right. This one didn't. It looked really stupid with Stella just wearing faded blue jeans and a tank top. "I couldn't look dumber if I wore black Sunday morning shoes and black socks while playing basketball, but mom can fix it later," she said into the mirror. She threw on a scarf and headed out to find Nate before lunch.

Stella rode her bike past Nate's house several times, but she couldn't bring herself to go knock on the door. Inside, she was burning with a desire to see if her guess was correct, that Nate was hiding because of something to do with how he looked. And she also wanted to remind Nate about the time spent in the closet and see in his eyes—without the sunglasses—if he felt the same way about her, that they had a secret relationship that they had never admitted to each other. And if that was also true, who knows what that might lead to.

Just before noon, Nate strolled out of his house and headed out for one of his walks toward the mall. Besides his heavy blue jeans, he was wearing almost all black. Stella rode up behind him and was about to say a cheery "hello" when the next-door-neighbor brat threw a firecracker just behind his feet. When it went off, in spite of the fact that Stella knew it must have surprised him, Nate just turned his head to stare once at the brat, spit, and he kept walking.

"Wow," Stella said as she biked up behind Nate, "that would have scared me purple." Nate stopped and gave a hint of a grin, then caught himself and went back to being serious.

"Scared me to death," he said smoothly, "but you can't let a skunk like that see you get scared or he'll do it again and tell everyone you're a scaredycat."

"You mean you can control yourself so much that you don't even show fear?"

"Sometimes," he replied.

"And what other things can you control so nobody knows about them?"

"What do you mean?"

"Like, these days you look like you don't care about your friends anymore. But what if that's just an act . . . like not showing how you feel about a firecracker?" Nate didn't say anything.

"What if, say, you don't swim anymore because, for instance, you don't like the way you look in a swimsuit?"

A look of surprise appeared suddenly on Nate's face, and he reached into his shirt pocket to pull out his sunglasses.

"Not so fast with those, Nathan," Stella said, grabbing the glasses first.

"Batman!" the neighborhood brat yelled as he jumped out from the bushes next to Stella and snatched the scarf from her head.

"Yuck!" yelled two of his brat-friends from the bushes. "Look at her hair. It's all twisted and backwards."

Stella tried to hide her hair in her hands.

Nate held his hand out for the scarf.

The brat pretended he was vomiting into the scarf as he said, "Barf-head, she's a barf-head."

Nate whipped the scarf out of his hand and snapped his fingers in front of the kid's face. "No names," he said in a low, menacing tone. "You don't call people names like that ever again, OK?"

The boy could tell Nate was serious. "Uh, yeah, I mean, no, I won't," he said.

The brat left. Stella turned to Nate and said, "Have dumbheads like me called you names—like Skinny—too many times?"

Nate made a funny twist of his mouth but didn't answer.

"And instead of telling us off, you decided not to show how you feel?"

Nate nodded.

"That's it? That's really it?" Stella could scarcely believe she had hit the bulls-eye.

He nodded again. "How did you know that about me? I haven't told anybody."

"You mean you're so lonely this summer because of people like me calling you Skinny? Oh, Nate, I'm so sorry. I never really thought you were *too* skinny. You're just, you know, trim." Her voice began to quiver. "You'll look great in a couple of years when you fill out. Everybody fills out. I'm so sorry, Nate."

Then Stella began to cry. And Nate's resolve to keep his feelings inside melted; he started to cry a bit, too, but it felt good to him to cry this time. They hugged each other.

"You think so?" he asked with an open kind of hope in his eyes. It was the old Nate again.

"Think what?" Stella asked.

"Do you think I'll fill out?"

"I will if you will," she laughed. "But let's do it in different places."

"Now tell me the truth—or else!" Nate said teasingly to Stella. "How on earth did you really find this out? I want to know!" he demanded.

"Oh, some stars told me," Stella replied sweetly as she laid her bike down and started to walk with him.

"Ya, right," he scoffed.

"Say, Nate, do you remember the time we hid in the closet together?"

As they walked and talked, he reached over and took her hand.

Nate's prayer: Boy, is Stella something! How did she know how tall and skinny I felt? Did you tell her somehow? Thank you for sending me a friend who can see what is really in me even when others can't. Amen.

Action idea: Think of a person or a situation that you don't quite understand as well as you wish you did. Pray for God to be with you, then pull out some paper and a pencil and start writing what comes to mind. You might discover some interesting things like Stella did.

"Each one, as a good manager of God's different gifts, must use for the good of others the special gift he has received from God."
—1 Peter 4:10

•

"A real hero would give up his life to save us."
—The Blonde

Walll-ter!

The all-clear siren sounded for the third time before the people dared to come out of their houses and stores. They saw a calm 12-year-old Walter Bitty standing over the garbage can–sized bomb and holding the innocent-looking but deadly detonator over his head.

Police moved quickly to cordon off the intersection and keep the adoring crowd—mostly pretty, young girls—from crushing Walter with their gratitude.

"My hero defused the nuclear bomb!" one long-haired blonde swooned.

"*Your* hero," a redhead scoffed. "He's *my* hero."

The love-struck blonde flashed with anger and shoved the redhead against a big-bellied police officer with a large, fuzzy mustache.

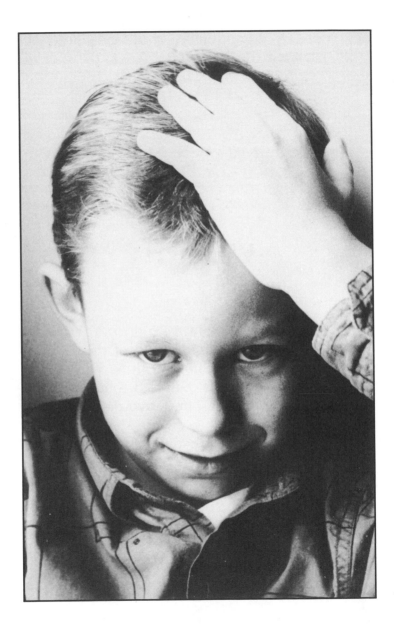

"Now, now, girls," the man said kindly, "don't fight. He's a hero for all time and for all people after what he did today."

The adoring crowd cheered wildly at that. "Walll-ter! Walll-ter!" they chanted. A newspaper photographer snapped a shot of Walter's triumphant pose.

Walter Bitty grinned sheepishly as he thought, *I'll remember this moment for as long as I live.*

The mayor and the chief of police stepped through the crowd and came towards Walter with smiles and extended hands. But the police chief stopped abruptly with his mouth frozen open. The timer on the detonator still glowed with luminous red numbers counting down on their way to zero. "It's still alive!" he shouted. "The bomb's defused, but the detonator is still alive!" The police chief turned and ran.

Walter realized that a detonator is really a small bomb used to set off a big bomb. The big bomb was safe, but. . . .

The glowing numbers counted down the seconds before detonation: "15 . . . 14 . . . 13. . . ."

The crowd panicked. "He's still got a bomb!" they shouted.

The mayor dashed for the nearest doorway. "10 . . . 9 . . . 8. . . ."

The crowd fled in all directions, screaming as they ran.

"Fall on the detonator," the mustachioed police officer called back to Walter as he dived behind a car. His voice was lost in the noise and confusion.

"A *real* hero would give up his life to save us," the blonde cried out.

"Yes, he should blow himself to itsy-bits to save us," the redhead agreed.

"This hero stuff is for the birds," Walter said. "There's no future in it."

"5 . . . 4. . . ."

Walter tossed the detonator to the street and ran.

"Walll-ter," the crowd called from all directions. "Don't leave us. Walll-ter, our hero. . . ."

"Walll-ter," the familiar voice called out. "Walll-ter! Come in for supper."

He skidded to a halt just short of vaulting the fence in his own backyard.

There were no pretty girls.

There was no crowd.

"But at least there's no detonator ready to go off," he said, wiping his forehead with the back of his hand. "Whew! Hero, schmero."

"Walll—oh, there you are," his mother said, coming around the corner. "My, my, you look like you've been chased by a bear," she said when she saw his frantic expression just starting to wear off. "More daydreams?"

Walter avoided her gaze. He knew his family considered him strange when he had his fantasies.

"No matter," she said kindly. "Now comb your hair and wash up. We're having liver and onions tonight."

"Liver!" he muttered, thinking his mother couldn't hear him. "I'll wash but I'm not combing my hair for no *liver*."

"Sorry, dear," she added, "I know I promised you hero sandwiches, but—"

"Hero! No hero here, thank you," he interrupted as he sprang up the back steps. His mother stood staring after him, then shrugged her shoulders and went in the house.

That night Walter thought the liver tasted better than usual.

●

Walter's daydreaming took a rest for a couple of days after that. But then he got a letter in the mail addressed to "Walty Bitter."

"Dear Walty," began the computerized form letter, trying to sound personal, "Junior high is just around the corner for you, and I'd like to invite you to the city-wide job fair which will be held next Saturday afternoon in the public library. It's for people just like you who are entering junior high in the fall. Come and meet people from many different occupations and dream about your own future."

It was signed by someone he had never heard of with the title "School District Career Guidance Counselor" after his name.

Putting the letter down, Walter felt a daydream coming on.

"Oh, Doctor Bitty," the blonde seventh grader began from the operating table, "you're so . . . so painless. I think I'll call you Doctor Painless."

Walter looked deeply into her eyes.

"That's because he hasn't started yet," the red-headed assistant doctor said dryly. "In your case, with all the things he's going to do with you, there will be *some* pain," she smiled, enjoying the look of fear on the blonde's face.

"Wrong!" Walter announced grandly. "I have invented and perfected two new tools that should give this young lady a pain-free operation."

"Operations, you mean," the red-haired doctor corrected. "She is here to have the works done, all the painful operations of her life done by you at one time."

"All of them?" Doctor Bitty replied incredulously. "Nobody's ever had *all* of them done at the same time."

"The works," his associate replied, "warts removed, ears pierced, appendix out, eyebrows plucked, bandage ripped off her scab, tonsils and adenoids out, then drillings and fillings, teeth straightened—he's a dentist too, you know—funny bone removed, color-blindness corrected, hangnails snipped, fourteen shots given for all diseases, and some stitches put in for a gash on her forehead."

"But my head's fine," the blonde patient argued.

"Fine for now, sure," the redheaded doctor replied, "but what if you hit your head on the edge of the pool?"

The blonde patient flinched and groaned.

"Worry not," Doctor Bitty called out gallantly as he yanked two shiny gizmos from his back pockets. "I have perfected my famous painless techniques.

Besides being a doctor and a dentist, I am a scientist, inventor, and toolmaker." He held the gizmos high over his head. A newspaper photographer stepped into the operating room and snapped a shot of Walter's triumphant pose.

"What's *he* doing in here?" the redhead demanded. "He's not scrubbed up."

"I'll escort him out of the operating room, Miss," said a big-bellied police officer with a large, fuzzy mustache.

"Where'd *you* come from?" the blonde asked from the table.

"Just doing my job protecting Doctor Walter here," was the reply. "He's so famous you never know who is going to ask him for his autograph or snap his picture."

Just then the double doors on the other side of the operating room burst open. Police moved quickly to cordon off the operating table and keep the adoring crowd—mostly pretty, seventh-grade girls—from crushing Walter with their gratitude. They started chanting, "Walll-ter, Walll-ter, Walll-ter. . . ."

"Walll-ter, why are you holding my can opener and egg whisk over your head?" his mother asked.

He quietly lowered his hands. *Caught again!* he realized.

"No matter," she continued. "Time to go to the dentist."

"Yeah, right . . . I mean, I knew that, Mom," he answered.

On the way to the car Walter asked, "Will it hurt?"

His mother replied, "I hear they call this guy Doctor Painless."

That afternoon Walter thought the dentist was more painful than usual.

•

The day for the job fair came and Walter was excited. Many of his friends thought it would be stupid and boring, but Walter thought maybe, just maybe, he could get some new ideas on what he wanted to be when he grew up. Something exciting, something where a lot of people would look up to him.

In my daydreaming I'm always wanting people to notice me, to see me as someone special, he realized, *but when they do, something always goes wrong. I'm not sure being famous is for me.*

His mother dropped Walter off at the library and called after him, "I'll be back at 3:00. I hope some of your friends come."

None of his closest friends came, so he felt like being a mouse in the corner for a while. He leaned against the far wall and just watched.

About twenty booths were set up where adults in various outfits and uniforms sat talking with some of the kids, perhaps over a hundred of them altogether. Some kids looked interested, some didn't seem to know how to start talking with the adults, and others looked like they were ready to go home.

Walter scanned the adults to see which ones seemed the most excited talking about their jobs. Some of the adults seemed as nervous as the kids, like they wanted to be noticed but couldn't come right out and say so. It reminded him of his daydreams when he wanted to be a hero or famous just so people would notice him.

"It's fun just watching people sometimes, isn't it, Walter?" a voice said from his right.

It was Pastor Salter from Walter's church.

"Yup," Walter replied.

"I like to watch people, too. It's my job to learn things about people."

"It is? What do you learn?"

"I learn what people are like, what they're likely to do."

"What do you mean?" Walter asked.

"Well, for instance, see that girl in the green skirt? Could be she just got her braces off. Look at how she makes a point of smiling just to show people. And the boy behind her seems embarrassed because his mother or father made him dress up with a tie and nobody else is wearing one."

As they watched, the boy slipped out of his tie and stuffed it in his hip pocket. The girl turned and smiled broadly at him, and he pointed with surprise at her mouth.

Walter laughed. "I'm impressed," he said.

"You try," Pastor Salter suggested.

Walter looked around the room. "OK," he began, "do you see those boys over there? They're trying not to act nervous," he said, pointing discretely. "And those two girls there think the new art teacher is cute, but they don't know if they should tell him or not."

"I think you're right about both," Pastor Salter said.

"So why are you here?" Walter asked.

"Same reason the other adults are," he answered.

"Trying to talk someone into becoming a pastor?"

"Nah, I leave that to God. I'm just here in case God has been talking to someone and they have some questions about the ministry to ask me."

Walter felt like he should have some questions, but he didn't.

Sensing this, Pastor Salter said, "I'm not trying to get you to become a pastor, Walter. That's not why I came over here to talk with you."

Walter quit furrowing his dark eyebrows.

"No," Pastor Salter continued, "but I am going to try to get you to do *something*."

"Like what?" Walter asked.

"I know you dream about what you will be some-day," he began.

Walter looked at him sharply like he had discovered his deep, dark secret. "You know?" Walter asked.

"Sure, everybody dreams."

Walter sighed.

Pastor Salter continued, "I just want you to plan your future, asking God to help you know what to do. And later, ask God to help you do whatever it is you are to do. God may ask you to be a pastor. It's a wonderful way to go through life, and it's much, much more exciting than most people realize. But God may call you to do and be something else. Look at all the occupations represented in this room."

Walter looked out over the crowd.

"God could call you to be any of these, or something else that isn't represented here. But the best thing for you, Walter, is to be where God wants you to be—no matter what that is."

Later that day, Walter daydreamed. He imagined that he had his hands up once again in a victory sign, but this time there were no people around to snap his picture, there was nobody with a large, fuzzy mustache; there wasn't even a crowd of seventh-grade girls. Nobody was noticing him at all. But then he noticed that God was noticing him. And he felt good.

Walter's prayer: Pastor Salter said he thinks I'm pretty good at noticing things about people. And since that job fair I've been noticing you, God, more and more when I'm at church—and even when I'm not at church. This is kind of a new thing for me. And by the way God, I won't say no right now to the possibility of being a pastor someday. Pastor Salter made it seem more exciting than I thought it would be, but you have to tell me a little more about it, OK? In Jesus' name, Amen.

Action idea: Talk to your pastor this week about what your pastor likes best about the job. Ask questions like: Do you have more chances to learn things about people and notice things about God than in most jobs? How does that make your life more interesting? Then ask your pastor how you can find out what God's will is for you. Chances are your pastor will *love* the chance to talk about these things with you!

"God made the wild animals . . . , the
livestock . . . , and all the creatures. . . . And God
saw that it was good."
—Genesis 1:24-25

•

*"Lick, lick. I always lick when something hurts.
Licking helps almost anything."*
—*Duke the Dog*

Duke the Dog

Dum dee dum, dum, dum.

Master is coming home soon. It's starting to cool
off, and I can smell squirrels starting to scamper
around the porch after the heat of the day.

I'm going to throw a little scare into them—
"WOOF!" That showed 'em. Dum dee dum, dum,
dum.

If I wander around the house just one more time,
I'll bet Master will be home. Goody, goody, I can't
wait.

Look at that, every time I think about Master my
tail just can't stop wagging. Aren't tails great? *Snap!*
Boy, I almost got that fly on my tail. I wonder why
I do that, though. Once I actually caught a fly in my
mouth and it tasted like—*Snap!*

One more look around the house. Oh, but I hate to get off my pillow next to the fan. But here goes. Dum dee dum, dum, dum.

Living room's in order. *Sniff, sniff.* Oops, I had an accident on the carpet here once; I had forgotten about that one. Good Master showed me I did wrong. Then he was so sad because he had to talk to me so angrily, and I had to go cheer him up afterwards. Master is so nice; there goes that tail again.

Is there anything under that sofa again? It seems like a food place. Ah, I remember finding a mushy baby cookie there once. Dum dee dum, dum, dum. Good cookie, but baby cried.

I'll save the kitchen for last. Now to the sleeping rooms.

Dum dee dum, dum, dum. Oh, this is Master's room. I can smell him all over the room. Nice Master scratches my ears better than anybody in the whole world. Then he scratches down my spine and spends a little extra time just when he gets to the tail. *Wonderful* Master. Nobody else takes the time to do that. Only Master. Makes me itch just thinking about it. *Scratch, scratch.* When is Master coming home? I hear a car . . . but it's the wrong sound.

Dum dee dum, dum, dum. The other sleeping rooms are boring compared to Master's sleeping room. I can sleep anywhere I want in Master's room. In the other rooms the people say "Go away" and "Get out."

Here's the kitchen. Dum dee dum, dum, dum. *Sniff, sniff.* Anything on the floor? Anything on the table? Oops. Master always says, "Get off the table! Get off the table! Get off the table!" There's an ant! *Snap, snap!* Missed him. I'm not too good at flies and ants anymore.

Stop and listen. Huh? There it is! A low, dark hum, shifting gears, it's that yellow bus! Master! Woof, woof! Woof, woof!

Master, Master, Master.

Run, run, dum dee dum, dum, dum. Will he want to do tricks? Will he want to play? He always gets me a biscuit to eat right away. Great! And he scratches so good.

Here he comes up the steps. Master! Woof! I'm here waiting for you. I've missed you all day. Woof, woof!

Run around the kitchen, chase my tail, act like I'm a puppy again. I just love it when Master comes home.

The door's open! Woof! Master! It's him and he's going for a biscuit. I just love Master.

But what's wrong? Master seems sad. Oh, oh. Bad day at that school? Oh, Master, I'll eat the biscuit later. Whimper, whimper. Does that make you feel better? *Lick, lick.* Now he's petting me like he's sad. Oh, Master. I'll jump on your lap. *Lick, lick.*

I'll put my head next to your neck. Oh, Master hugged me. *Lick, lick.* I always lick when something hurts. Licking helps almost anything.

He's starting to smile. Dum dee dum, dum, dum. Master just needed a hug and about ten good licks. Right, Master? Woof?

Woof!

He wants to play—outside! Great! Woof, woof! Where's that ball, where's that ball? *Sniff, sniff, sniff.* In the closet over here, Master. When I scratch on the door he remembers where it is.

Master is wonderful.

I love Master better than anything else in the whole world because Master loves Duke the Dog.

That's me!

Woof!

Master's prayer: Thank you, God, for my dog, Duke. He's always waiting for me and treating me like I'm the most important person in the whole world. Maybe I am the most important person in his world. When I come home sad or tired or angry, just being with him makes me relaxed and happy. I don't know what it is about a good dog that does that to me. I guess it's because dogs like Duke just love you no matter what. Thanks for Duke. Amen.

Action idea: Every kind of love can teach us something about God's love for us. The love between a boy and his dog can be very special. Ask yourself some questions:

- How is the boy's love in the story like God's love for us?
- How is Duke's love for the Master like worship?
- Who showed unconditional love (love that is just there without having to be earned) in the story?

"If we claim to be without sin, we deceive
ourselves and the truth is not in us."
—1 John 1:8

•

*"My parents both tell us we shouldn't admit any
weakness or sin so we can become perfect."*
—Mary Anne

An Eye on the Gibbons

Joe had his eye on the Gibbons. And it was not
just in church on Sundays when they sat in "their
pew," second from the front on the right, precisely
in front of the pulpit. Nobody ever, ever sat in front
of them. But Joe wasn't sure if that was because you
had to pay extra attention sitting right in front of
the preacher or because the Gibbons seemed just too
much better than everyone else. In church *everyone*
had their eyes on the Gibbons. Starched shirts and
bright blouses, hair fashioned and fluffed, hands
folded on ironed laps and the kind of smiles you
would expect from the *perfect* family.

Joe had his eye on the Gibbons for another reason.
And it was not just because 12-year-old Mary Anne
was a radiant replica of her mother, who many said
had been the prettiest Miss Seattle ever. Mary Anne

had hair the color of fine sand, ocean blue eyes, and a permanent tan. Though she seemed always to move carefully and gracefully, her flitting gaze gave evidence of a quick mind. That gaze had caught Joe looking at her too many times. Always she smiled and he looked away.

Joe had his eye on the Gibbons for lots of reasons, but the main one was that they bothered him and he didn't know why.

•

Mary Anne was a front-of-the-classroom kind of person; she was in the top reading group since first grade. But she was quiet on the playground when there were no adults around. For all these reasons and more Joe hadn't really gotten to know her well until summer school following sixth grade.

"I'd like five volunteers to paint the backdrop for our play," Mr. Bourne said on the first day of class. "It'll take some extra afternoon hours early on, but you'll be done early, too, when the others are scheduled for extra play rehearsals. Okay, I see five hands. Who wants to be the chairperson of this art committee? How about Mary Anne? Fine."

Of course Mary Anne, Joe thought. *The teacher knows anything she does turns out perfect.*

On the first afternoon of work on the backdrop, Mary Anne led the other four painters and Mr. Bourne to a remote hallway that was seldom used.

"Why, Mary Anne," Mr. Bourne crowed, "you've already rolled out newsprint on the floor."

"It's triple thickness so the paint doesn't leak through, and it's taped together to make a surface six feet by fifteen feet, perfect for the stage in the small gym."

Mr. Bourne looked troubled. "That's what I would have suggested. But Mary Anne, you've already sketched the scenery. That was to have been done by this committee."

"You don't like it?" Mary Anne asked incredulously.

"My goodness, not that. It's perfect."

There's that word again, Joe thought. *Perfect!*

Mr. Bourne continued, "It's just that everyone should have had a chance to . . . well, never mind. This will be fine; it's really quite attractive. You must have worked on it—"

"—All weekend," Mary Anne finished. She looked relieved. "We wanted it to look nice. My parents both helped me to design and sketch this."

Joe had that funny feeling about the Gibbons again.

"OK, there's the paint. Pick a color and go," Mr. Bourne said. "I'll check back in half an hour."

Joe painted tree trunks. Mary Anne painted leaves. They finally talked.

"Going anywhere on vacation this summer?" she asked Joe.

"Nope. You?"

53

"Yes. We're flying to see some of the summer Olympics."

"Figures," Joe said, then wished he hadn't when he saw Mary Anne's expression.

"What do you mean by that?" she asked.

"Sorry. Didn't mean anything by it. I guess you Gibbons are always doing the perfect thing. Going to the Olympics is pretty special."

"You're just jealous," she chided. "Besides, we might not go at all; my sister's sick, sort of."

"Mary Anne!" her mother's voice interrupted as she stepped past two other painters.

"Oh, hi, Mother. We won't be done for an hour. Stop back then, will you?" Mary Anne looked uncomfortable. "Please."

"What happened to our lovely birch trees? They *were* birch trees, weren't they, dear? Isn't that what we planned over the weekend? These birch trees aren't white like they should be."

Mary Anne gave Joe an apologetic look. He suddenly realized that he was going to be drawn into the conversation.

"Mom, this is Joe. He decided to paint brown maple tree trunks instead of white birch tree trunks."

Joe started to explain, "I really didn't know about—"

"Well, ask him to do those two trunks over or you'll have to redo a hundred leaves. You're not painting maple leaves, you know, honey."

"Nobody will notice," Joe blurted out.

"Don't be silly," Mrs. Gibbon replied. "*We* will notice." She looked suspiciously at Joe. "Maybe you should do those trunks over yourself, Mary Anne, to make sure they are done right. Besides, you *are* the chairperson. Mr. Bourne put a star by your name. . . ."

"Oh, Mother!" Mary Anne wailed with a sour tone.

Mrs. Gibbon looked like she had been slapped. Looking at the platoon of young workers, she said, "Honey, don't talk to me like that in front of your little friends. Your father will have a few words with you later."

The click of her heels and the smell of her sweet perfume lingered long after she was gone. The other painters decided to go for a drink of water.

"I'm sorry, Joe," Mary Anne finally said.

"I'll do them over when the paint is dry," he offered.

"Don't. What you did is just fine."

"But they'll notice," he said.

"They notice *everything!* There's no pleasing them," Mary Anne said softly. Tears formed in the bottoms of both ocean-blue eyes. She leaned closer to Joe and asked, "Promise you'll keep a secret?"

Joe leaned slightly away. "I guess so. I mean, sure."

"My older sister is sick with anorexia. That means she won't eat and has lost too much weight. She can't help it."

Joe didn't know how to respond. He looked down at the pattern of the tiles in the floor.

"The doctor says my parents may have been part of the cause by expecting us to be too perfect."

That word again!

"And so we're all going into family counseling. You can't tell anyone, or my mom and dad will be too embarrassed. We're not going to go to church for a while until Connie's well again."

Joe felt like he was in the way. But at least now he knew what was different about the Gibbons. They were special people, shining people, sometimes perfect people. But they felt they had to shine all the time, like leaving a light turned on all night *and* all day. Makes the bulb burn out quicker. Makes Mary Anne's sister get sick. And what about Mary Anne?

"I guess you didn't ask to know all of this," Mary Anne said. "I feel silly for telling you. It's just that I'm . . . I'm scared I'm going to get sick too . . . and I don't know what to do about it."

With that, Mary Anne threw her arms around Joe and cried silently but with heaving shoulders.

Joe wondered if he could have been as honest about something that hard. This was a side to Mary Anne that he couldn't have imagined. He cried some too, but with his eyes open. He hoped the three other painters would just keep walking down the hall with their backs turned.

Mary Anne sniffed on his shoulder, looked up, and said, "I'm all right now. *Sniff.* I'll just pray— *Sniff*—that God will make me more perfect. *Sniff, sniff.*"

"I don't want to tell you what to do or anything," Joe began, "but I don't think you could be any more perfect than you already are."

Mary Anne brightened a bit and tried to smile.

"What I mean is, you really try so hard with everything, and who says you have to be perfect anyway?"

"Mom told us the Bible says we are to be perfect as our heavenly Father is perfect. My parents both tell us we shouldn't admit any weakness or sin so we can become perfect. I believe them because they're really strong Christians."

"I didn't think church was a place to go to act perfect all the time," Joe said. "I thought that was where we went to admit that we *weren't* perfect and that we need God's help. If we had to be perfect to be Christians, *poof!* I'd be gone right now. I like the *real* you better than the *perfect* you anyway."

This time it was Mary Anne's turn to be speechless. But she wasn't looking at the floor tiles. She was looking right at Joe, and the glint in her ocean blue eyes said it all.

Joe's prayer: Dear God, am I ever glad we don't have to try to be perfect in order for you to like us. Look at how unhappy it made Mary Anne! Now that I know how hurting her family is, help me not to feel uncomfortable around them anymore. And don't let them stop coming to church—so I can see Mary Anne on the weekends too! Amen.

Action idea: In the next few days (or hours), someone in your family is likely to make a mistake in front of you. Be ready to say quickly, "That's all right. God still loves you and so do I." You might just make them smile.

57

"God saw what they did and how they had turned
from their evil ways."
—Jonah 3:10

•

*"There's a man . . . out there . . . and he has a
gun . . . and he's looking for . . . YOU,"*
—Andy

The Zero

Somewhere below the lower reaches of the "Geek" there lives a "Zero." His name is Andy.

Andy was not always called a "Zero."

He was born into a family that was not able to have any other children. He was much more than a "Zero" to his parents. They loved their bright-eyed little baby as much as anyone has ever loved a baby. He was such a pretty baby that many people thought the parents ought to have him do television commercials. But they were content to keep him at home and love him and take care of him.

Andy was three when his mother died in a car accident. The driver who hit her survived the crash without even a broken bone because he was so limp from being drunk. Andy's father tried to keep his job *and* take care of his young son. That lasted a year.

When Andy was four years old, his father went into the hospital for surgery and Andy went to live with his godparents in the next state. The arrangement was supposed to be temporary, but somehow his father's health never allowed him to take Andy back. Andy's godparents, like many godparents at the time a baby is born, had promised to raise Andy if it was ever necessary. But they weren't all that happy when it really happened. They hadn't counted on having five children of their own by the time Andy moved in with them.

By the time Andy was in first grade, teachers were calling him "hyperactive." He couldn't sit and pay attention very well when the librarian read books to the class, he talked too fast and too loud out of turn, and he got yelled at a lot by adults who didn't know about Andy's background.

By second grade, Andy was being sent to other parts of the school for special classes. He was called a "problem child." His godparents were trying to restrict his diet—especially red food dye—but when some kids at school found out about Andy's special food needs, they would bring him red licorice on the playground just to see what would happen.

Andy was adopted by his godparents when he was in the fourth grade. By this time he was old enough to understand what this meant. His father had gotten remarried to a woman with four kids of her own, but even so Andy couldn't figure out why his father didn't want him to come and live with him. His father told him it was because he had been raised by his godparents and they were his real parents now. Then his father moved to the east coast, hundreds of miles away. He was teased by kids at school that his father "didn't want him."

When Andy was in the seventh grade, the family got hooked up with a church for the first time—sort of. Andy's adoptive parents decided all the children would be picked up for Sunday school at a local church so they could sleep a bit later at least one morning a week. They worked hard and thought they had it coming. Besides, the parents said, they had to go through all that "religious stuff" when they were growing up, so the kids had to, too. They made it sound like punishment.

That's when Andy met Mrs. Fontana.

Mrs. Fontana didn't know anything at all about Andy Becker that first Sunday of the school year. The members of the class who arrived early didn't recognize the name, either, when she asked them about Andy.

"What if it's a *really* cute skateboarding boy from California," Heather ventured with a tilt to her head, "who just moved to town and doesn't know anybody yet?"

"Hey," Benji suggested, "I think that might be the new guy who placed in the junior nationals in long-distance running. He's cool."

"An athlete?" Amy asked. "Is he tall or strong or what?"

"I don't know," Benji said. "I just heard he's amazing."

"Just what this boring town needs," Heather swooned, "a little more 'amazing.' "

Just then, as if on cue, Andy came running around the corner into the classroom like he was being chased. With fast breathing and a frantic look on his face, he blurted out loudly, "There's a man . . . out there . . . and he has a gun . . . and he's looking for . . . *YOU!*" As he said this, he whipped around and pointed at Heather.

Heather shrieked.

The rest of the class froze.

Mrs. Fontana got up from the class table and edged her way toward the door. Heather whimpered, Jeff muttered, and the other five kids sat rigid with mouths hanging open.

Just as Mrs. Fontana got to the door and started to peek into the hallway, Heather pulled herself together enough to say, "Wait a minute, how do you know he's after *me*? I don't even know you."

Mrs. Fontana, having checked the hallway thoroughly, turned slowly with a smile on her face and said, "Mr. Andrew Becker, I presume."

"Is he gone? Is he gone?" Andy said quickly. "Then it's time for Sunday school, isn't it?" With that, Andy picked up the huge Bible on the stand next to the chalkboard and dropped it on the table with a tremendous *SLAP!* Everyone jumped. Then Andy sat at the only free chair and folded his hands expectantly on the table in front of him.

Mrs. Fontana picked up the big Bible and took her seat again.

Benji realized first who he was. "Hey, it's the Zero from school."

"Hey, Zero-man, I didn't recognize you with your hair combed," said another boy.

Heather looked miffed. "You mean there's no athlete? There's no California skateboarder? There's just this . . . this . . . one minus one? This less-than-a-Geek?"

"Let's ask an expert Geek. Delbert here is a Geek," Amy said of the boy sitting to her right. "Isn't that right, Delbert?"

"Is Andy even less than you, Delbert?" Heather asked. "That must take the pressure off you to be so—"

"Are you girls about done?" Mrs. Fontana asked. "If so, it seems the class members are all here now and we can begin."

"All right, Mrs. Fontana," Heather said.

"Sorry, Mrs. Fontana; sorry, Delbert," Amy said.

"Eek, a Geek!" said Andy, pointing at Delbert.

●

Andy came to Sunday school every week all fall, to Heather's great consternation.

On one Sunday, he pulled off all the "fairy loops" on the backs of the shirts the boys were wearing. Benji's "fairy loop" didn't let go, so his shirt ripped all the way down to his waist.

Another Sunday, he handed out dental floss and showed everyone how to get the "muck" out from between the teeth. "I'm going to raise dental floss in Montana some day," Andy said as he puffed out his chest. "Yup, going to make my first fortune raising dental floss—or maybe in raising sugar cane. My dad says I'm good at raising cane. Get it?"

Every week it was something. Bizarre homemade stickers that showed "nude fish" going to church. A squirt gun filled with disappearing ink that didn't exactly disappear. Wanting to play "hangman" using only four-letter words.

Delbert was really the only one in the class who didn't mind Andy. Andy's antics as Zero-man made Delbert's title, Geek, almost disappear. Delbert felt almost freed from his Geek prison on Sunday mornings.

Heather, on the other hand, was usually the first one Andy turned to with his practical jokes, ever since that first day when he had pointed at her as the one the supposed gunman was seeking. Heather went so far as to ask her parents if she could quit Sunday school because of Andy. Failing that, she talked with the Sunday school superintendent about the fact that she should have flunked last year and should really still be in the sixth grade. He didn't buy that story. Heather was stuck.

Mrs. Fontana made it teaching through the fall by throwing out her normal lesson plans and choosing activities and discussions that were faster paced. These held Andy's attention better, and the students had to admit classes became more interesting than they used to be. They just took the teacher much more time to prepare.

But Mrs. Fontana didn't seem to mind. In fact, she saw Andy as a gift to the class, someone with a truly unique perspective on things.

This came out in the many discussions. When most kids would say what they thought Mrs. Fontana wanted to hear, Andy would say whatever came into his head.

"How many of the twelve apostles can you name?" Mrs. Fontana asked.

"All twelve," Andy said.

"Well, Andy is going to try to remember their names, and the rest of the class will try to get any he leaves out. Go, Andy."

"Easy," Andy said, and he began, "Peter, James, John, Flopsy, Mopsy, Cottontail, Comet, Cupid, ah, Rudolph, Mo, Curly, Batman, Robin, and, of course, the Beaver."

"Andy got three of the most important ones, class."

"The rabbits, Mrs. Fontana?" Heather asked.

"No, Peter, James, and John. What are the names of the others?"

By this time, the others were so hyped and motivated by Andy's efforts that they actually succeeded in naming all but one of the others, and in the process named Bo Jackson, Michael Jackson, and Stonewall Jackson besides.

"What happens to us after we die, class?" Mrs. Fontana asked in the middle of another lesson.

At that, Andy grabbed Delbert by the throat and pretended he was choking him. Delbert played along. After Delbert was "dead," Andy got three others to help him "bury" Delbert by covering him with some handy newsprint. Then Andy designated the supply cabinet heaven and they lifted Delbert to a perch where he swayed near the ceiling.

Mrs. Fontana knew that her planned lesson was shot, so she allowed the kids to continue the spontaneous drama.

Andy then turned to Heather: "Officer, I confess. I did it. Lock me up." Officer Heather was overjoyed. She led Andy back to the supply cabinet and shut him in "jail."

"Doesn't he get a trial?" Benji asked. "Even Andy should get a trial. Knock twice if you want a trial, Andy."

Knock. Knock.

"There, see? I get to be the judge," Benji claimed.

"I'll be the prosecuting attorney," Amy said gleefully.

"Who will defend me?" came a voice from the cabinet.

Silence.

"Someone?"

"I can't; I'm dead and gone, Andy," said Delbert from atop the cabinet.

"I know, I killed you," said Andy.

Mrs. Fontana finally said, "Well, if nobody will volunteer, I'll defend him. But I'll defend him using the Bible. Any objections?"

"This court is in session," Benji said.

Two of the other boys dragged Andy from the cabinet and propped him in a chair in front of Judge Benji.

"What do you have to say for yourself?" Benji intoned.

"I killed him with these two hands and if I could reach him up there on the cabinet, I'd do it again right now," was Andy's response.

"It doesn't look good, Mrs. Fontana," Benji said.

"But Your Honor," she said, "he's no more guilty of murder than any of the other people here."

"That's not true," objected Heather. "We saw him kill Delbert."

"Ah, but you agreed to use the Bible for this trial, and it says, right here, in Matthew chapter five, 'You have heard that people were told in the past, "Do not commit murder; anyone who does will be brought to trial." But now I tell you: whoever is angry with his brother will be brought to trial. . . .' "

Andy lit up. "You've all been angry with me, haven't you? Haven't you?"

"Does it really say that, Mrs. Fontana?" Judge Benji asked. "You wouldn't lie to us, would you?"

"No, and furthermore it says in Romans chapter three, 'There is no one who is righteous, no one who is wise or who worships God. All have turned away from God; they have all gone wrong; no one does what is right, not even one.' "

"So we're all guilty, then," Heather said. "Well, as prosecuting attorney, I suggest to the judge that *everybody* be put on trial for murder."

"Granted," the judge said. "But now we need a new judge since I'm on trial too.

"God is our only true judge," a voice from the door said. It was Mr. Jenkins, the Sunday school superintendent. "And since I've watched most of this most unusual class already, and each of you is playing other parts, I get to be God. Who wants to go first?"

"Well, I haven't missed a Sunday school class all year," Amy said.

"Not good enough to offset the sin," Mr. Jenkins said sternly.

"I'm not a goofball in class like Andy here," Heather said.

"Sorry," said "God." "You're not judged in comparison to others, only according to God's law."

The kids were talking quietly among themselves trying to decide how to save themselves when a voice from the top of the supply cabinet spoke up, "Excuse me, may I speak?"

"You're dead up there," "God" said.

"No, I'm in heaven, God, remember?"

"Oh, all right. What do you have to add to these proceedings?"

"Well, you know I'm in heaven and all . . . and Jesus is up here, of course . . . and I was talking with him the other day and he said, well, that all these people know him." Delbert felt good about his little speech.

"That's not good enough. A lot of people know my son," "God" said.

"But it's more than that," Delbert added. "Jesus says they're his friends and even his brothers and sisters."

"They are?"

The whole class and Mrs. Fontana nodded.

"Well, then," "God" said, "Not guilty!"

"Whew!" the teacher said. "That was a good thing you thought of, Delbert. Whatever made you think of it?"

"I got to thinking that most of the time it's not *what* you know, but *who* you know that counts," Delbert said.

"That's right; who, who, who," Andy called out in his best barn owl imitation.

"From now on, no more Geek talk about Delbert if I'm around," Benji said, pledging to protect him from name calling.

"So, another good ending to a weird class—although not one I had planned," Mrs. Fontana said.

"And to think we could have had a *normal* Sunday school class if Andy hadn't joined us," Heather said. "How boring. Think of all the stupid fun we would have missed."

"Yeah, we're glad you're in our class, Andy," Benji said.

Andy took a bow, then he took about twenty more.

"Can somebody help me down?" said a voice from "heaven."

Andy's prayer: Dear God, dear God, dear God, dear God. Oh, boy, oh, boy, oh, boy, oh, boy. Fun class, fun class, fun class, fun class. They like me, they like me, they like me, they like me. Amen, amen, amen, amen.

Action idea: Ask your pastor or the Sunday school superintendent at your church whether someone like Andy would be welcome at Sunday school. (Many churches say they don't have students with special needs like Andy. Maybe they don't have those students because they don't offer the space or curriculum that they need.)

"Whoever calls his brother 'You good-for-nothing!' will be brought before the Council."
—Matthew 5:22

•

"You think I wouldn't call a Chicano a spic? It's no different than calling a Black a nigger or an Asian a chink. They all know that's what they are."
—Sammy

Steak

"Do you really think we ought to tell the kids?" Mr. Taylor said in a mock whisper to his wife.

She played along as usual. "They're going to find out anyway; it might as well be from us instead of from Doc."

Griff got excited. He put his drumstick down mid-chomp. Whenever his parents played this game between them, it always turned out to be very good news.

Teri gasped. "Mother! You're not! You're too old!"

The three younger girls tittered and prodded and demanded, "She's not what, Teri? Too old for what, Teri?"

"I'll give you a hint," their father said. "She didn't mean a doctor. She meant Doc Piper."

Teri slumped with relief but hastened to add, "I didn't really mean that you were *old* old, Mother. Just too, you know, too old to have a baby."

"A baby!" two of the other girls shrieked.

Dawn, the youngest, started to cry. "I'm the baby," she blubbered.

"No more babies," Mrs. Taylor said with a firm look at her husband.

Griff was a boy of few words. But he shared a few at that moment and everyone, as usual, paid attention.

"A pet," he said simply. "We're getting a pet."

"You're close, Griffin," his dad said. "But still no cigar. After supper what say we head over to Doc Piper's farm and meet the newest member of this family?"

"Can she come home with us tonight?" Emily asked.

"It's a he, and your dad shouldn't have said it's part of the family. This particular he doesn't have long to live," Mrs. Taylor said.

"You'll see," Mr. Taylor said. "Let's finish and I'll explain it all out at the farm."

●

Doc Piper took pride in all the "critters" on his farm. Walking across the barnyard, he pointed out two loping dogs coming in from the field, the pecking chickens near the coup, a few ducks by the water tank. As the younger kids heard him introduce the animals, their eyes got bigger and bigger with expectation. When they all rounded the corner of the machine shed and saw a mother horse with a colt, they almost didn't hear Doc Piper say, "And this new colt is for my grandchild."

"Then which animal is ours?" Emily asked.

"That fellow over there looks like he's expecting you," was Doc's reply.

"A cow?" Dawn asked. "He'll have to sleep in Griff's room since he's a boy cow."

"A boy cow is called a steer," Doc said. "And this guy is going to have to live with me on the farm until—"

"Until we build a house for him?" Emily asked hopefully.

Doc looked somberly at Mr. Taylor. "You didn't tell them?"

"I told you not to let them think he—I mean it—was a pet," Mrs. Taylor said.

Griff understood. "We're going to eat that guy some day."

"Don't be gross, Griff," Teri scolded. "You'll scare the little ones."

He enjoyed making his sisters squirm so he continued. "You heard about Old MacDonald who had a farm?"

Dawn chimed in, "E-I-E-I-O."

"Well," Griff continued, "what do you think he did with all his cows and steers after he quit farming?"

He was met with blank stares.

"First Old MacDonald built some golden arches, and then he bought a stove and started making hamburgers—billions and billions of them."

His story had its desired effect on the little ones.

"Dad, stop Griff from scaring the girls," Teri demanded.

"Well, his story is a bit far-fetched, but he's right about that steer out there," Mr. Taylor said. "One year from today he's going to be in our freezer."

"What are you going to call him?" Doc asked.

"Let's have a contest," Emily suggested.

●

The next evening, each of the kids entered one name and one name only for the contest.

Dawn liked Spot.

Teri tried to reason with her. "But he doesn't have any spots like the dog in the book."

"It don't matter," she pouted. "He's not a dog anyway."

"It makes a strange sort of sense," Mrs. Taylor said. "Let's not criticize each other's names."

"Well, I like the name Griff," said 6-year-old Michelle, who was usually quiet like her older brother. She gave him another of her patented you're-my-hero looks.

"Yuck! Could you eat a cow named Griff? We're not cannibals, Michelle," Emily burst out in disgust.

"What's that?" little Dawn asked brightly.

"Mom and Dad play tennis with a can-o'-balls," Griff said.

"Quick thinking," Teri whispered to him.

Emily took center stage with, "Let's name him Bambi."

"Dumbo is more like it," Teri said. "He's going to be huge by next year."

"Oh, yeah? And what's your choice?" Emily snapped.

"I don't have one. I think that this whole thing is stupid because if we name that steer anything, it will be like killing and eating a pet next year."

"I have the solution." Griff looked confident.

"This is the last entry in the contest," his mother said. "After this, we all vote. Go ahead, Griffin."

"We call him Steak. With a name like that, it will be easy to do anything we want with him next year."

"Ah, now there's a name for you," Mr. Taylor said. "I like mine medium rare."

"With mushrooms," Teri added.

"And baked potatoes with sour cream," said Mrs. Taylor.

"I liked it when we had steak fondue," Emily said.

Mr. Taylor said, "Sounds like we have a winner here. All in favor of calling him Steak raise your right hand—Dawn, that's your left—then Steak it is. Way to go, Griff!"

●

School had started and Griff was walking home with Tom and Sammy.

"Hey, we got a second spic in our class this year," Sammy said as he kicked the garbage basket on the street sign post. "Let's call him Span. Get it? We can call them Spic and Span." He was the only one laughing at his joke.

"Yeah, I'd like to see you call José a spic to his face," Tom said. "I don't think you'd dare."

Griff decided to stay out of the conversation for the time being.

"You think I wouldn't call a Chicano a spic? It's no different than calling a Black a nigger or an Asian a chink. They all know that's what they are."

Griff wanted very badly not to be out in public with Sammy just then. He didn't like Sammy even on good days, though they were both friends with Tom. "Come on, Sammy," Griff motioned. "You can't go around talking like that."

"Don't be such a jerk, Griff," was his reply.

"Don't start calling me names, Sammy," Griff challenged.

"Jerk doesn't like being called a jerk?" Sammy said as he advanced on Griff and shoved him against the garbage basket.

Griff, never easily flustered or drawn into an argument, said to Tom, "He's your friend, buddy. You can have him."

But before Griff walked away from his first fight, he turned and said to Sammy, "Tell me something. When you call someone a bad name, it makes it easier to hurt them, doesn't it?"

Sammy shrugged with a tough look. "So?"

Steak

"You call them spic or nigger or jerk and they almost seem to deserve anything you can dish out. Right?"

"Get out of here, jerk," was Sammy's reply.

Griff's prayer: God, I was the one who named the steer Steak so it would be easier to kill him later. When I see how some people do the same thing to other people, it makes me want to vomit. Sorry, I don't suppose you want to hear about vomit in my prayers. Well, you probably don't want to hear about kids like Sammy, either. Open his eyes to see what a stupid thing he's doing. And if you ever catch me about to call people names like that, stop me. I won't mind. Amen.

Action idea: Think of all the bigoted, hateful names you can. If you used all those ugly names to make enemies with the world's five billion people, how many people would be left? Wouldn't it be lonely?

"Do nothing out of selfish ambition or vain
conceit."
—Philippians 2:3

•

*"I couldn't afford a bigger allowance. If it was
bigger, I couldn't blackmail my folks any time I
want like that, could I? Ya learnin' anything here,
Willie?"*
—Spencer

Top Top Dog

Willie took notes as he watched a cluster of the
"beautiful people" of his junior high school. Willie
was trying to figure out how these kids were different
from the rest. He wanted to become one of them
and, like the top-notch science student he was, he
began by observing. The experimentation and new
discoveries would come later.

"The group is boys and girls, short and tall, black
and white, but they're all dressed *sharp*." *So far so
good*, thought Willie who was tall, black, and trying
to dress better. "The girls hit the guys a lot when
they tease," he continued writing in his notebook,
"but the guys can only poke the girls in return.
Tickling is all right for anyone to do, except nobody

seems to even touch the 'Top Top Dog.' " The "Top Top Dog," as he came to know the cream of the cream, was Spencer.

Willie pulled a separate page out of his notebook and wrote "Spencer" at the top. *This guy deserves his own page,* Willie realized. He wrote, "Spencer keeps his arms folded and leans against things. When he leans against people, they don't move, not even to tease. Someone who moved would be seen as not one of them. Spencer also puts his floppy, expensive shoes up on things that adults tell us we shouldn't have our feet on, like the glass trophy case by the drinking fountain. It makes it look like he *owns* that trophy case and personally earned every trophy in it."

Willie shifted his position—observing the group for almost an hour after school from a concrete bench that had made his body stiff—and he wrote some more: "Spencer doesn't smile as much as the others, but when he does he laughs loud and then goes back to his wide-eyed, innocent-puppy look. That seems to be his look for when he's around girls. They love it. When he's around guys only, his face is different; it looks like he's been doing something he shouldn't have. He's a real wise guy around just guys. Spencer is like a chameleon. He can be what it takes to get people to think he's . . . he's . . . a what?"

Willie looked up once again at Spencer. Spencer finally seemed to notice the attention, even from fifty yards away with a large pane of glass between them.

But he quickly turned back to lean on a tall girl wearing lots of makeup.

Ah, what a life this guy's got, Willie thought. He tried on his own wide-eyed, innocent-puppy look, leaned against a concrete pillar, and said to an imaginary companion, "Spencer may be a year older than I am, and he has all the attention for now, but next year I'll be the eighth grader and he'll be gone. Then I'll be the new Spencer." Willie saw more hitting and poking and tickling and laughing—everybody trying to get Spencer's attention. "On the other hand, why wait until next year? I'm going to be you," he said in the direction of the Top Top Dog.

●

Willie was back at the concrete bench that had been his observation post after school for two weeks. Fortunately, the Top Dogs also had their one special place where they talked and impressed each other. Willie didn't have to follow them all over town.

As Willie laid out his notes, now in various colored pocket folders, he noticed that Spencer wasn't with the others today. He reached for the orange folder, marked "Top Top Dog," to make a note of this when suddenly he felt a heavy body leaning on his back.

"I know you," a voice said.

Spencer.

"No, I don't think you do," Willie said without moving.

"How would you know? You haven't looked around," Spencer said.

Willie turned around slowly, then said, "Nope, I was right, you don't know me."

"Sure, I do," Spencer insisted. "You're the guy who's been watching me and taking notes."

Willie was starting to get worried by the tone in Spencer's voice. "Me? Watching you?"

"Look, kid, I know when people are watchin' me. It's, like, the thing I do best. Ya gotta, if ya wanna know when the girls notice ya."

Realizing that he had been discovered, Willie pulled a sheet out of the orange file, tried to act as natural as possible, and wrote, "Knowing when people are watching is very important."

Spencer was intrigued. "Very good, kid, you got guts! You didn't back down. Now let me see that folder."

Spencer continued leaning on Willie as he read about himself. And he liked it. A lot.

After five minutes of reading, interrupted now and then by his asking Willie "What's this word?" he tossed the folder down with a satisfied expression.

"You're really learnin' somethin' watchin' me, ya know?" Spencer said.

"I know."

"What is this, then? A fan club?"

"No."

"Are you spyin' on me for somebody?"

"No."

"Look, kid, this ain't a game show. Tell me what you're doin'."

Willie hoped Spencer would respond best to the truth, so he said slowly, "I want . . . to be . . . like you." He thought it might make Spencer embarrassed, and Willie worried that an embarrassed Spencer might be an angry Spencer.

"So? Nothin' wrong with that," Spencer said easily. "A lot of guys want to be like me. That's 'cause I'm a 'Top Top Dog,' right?"

"You're not *a* Top Top Dog," Willie replied.

"What are you sayin'?" Spencer asked, his voice threatening.

"You are *the* Top Top Dog."

Spencer looked relieved and starting bobbing his head. "Sure. Okay. Right. I know. That's me. Well. All right. I know."

Willie knew he had made it past this first encounter with Spencer.

"I like that," Spencer said. "The *Top* Top Dog. You're all right, kid."

"Willie."

"Sure. Okay. Right. Willie. Say, Willie—that your name?—Willie, what if you didn't have to just watch me after school? What if I, like, taught ya a few things so as you could learn? What if I was sorta' your teacher? Hey, me a teacher! Wowwww!"

"Sure," Willie said without even thinking.

"Sure. Okay. Right," Spencer said.

"Okay. Right," Willie added.

"Now," Spencer said abruptly as he cuffed Willie's head. "Let's go. My house."

"Why your house?"

" 'Cause the Spencer you see here, the Top Top Dog, didn't get this way by accident. You wanna learn? I'll show ya. Come on."

At the porch of Spencer's house, he stopped momentarily to fill Willie in on his plans.

"All right. Now. The secret to understanding adults is money. Right?"

Willie nodded.

"And the secret to understanding money is not to want too much of it. Now, if you don't understand that, Willie—that your name?—you'll never get lots of it—money—and that's what we're after, right? Lots of money, 'cause money can buy things that make ya a Top Dog. Right? Ya got that?"

"Sure."

"Okay. Right. So watch how I can get money by not wanting money. Just watch me. Hey, Ma!" Spencer put on his wide-eyed, innocent-puppy look and went in the house with Willie following. "Ma!" He turned to whisper to Willie. "The Look," he pointed to his face, "works with adults better than it works with girls."

Willie thought Spencer's mother looked so ordinary to have a son like Spencer.

"Hi, dear," she said. "Did you bring home one of your little friends?"

"Yeah, Ma, a little friend named, ah, Willie, Ma."

"Pleased to meet you, Willie."

84

"Same here," Willie said.

"Can I get you boys a snack?" she asked brightly.

"No, Ma, we're heading downtown 'cause, ah, Willie here's got to do some shoppin'. Ain't that right, Willie?"

Willie nodded.

"Now I don't have no money, Ma, and I'm not asking for much, just the 50 cents for next week's allowance if you can, like, give me an advance."

Spencer's mother looked embarrassed as she grabbed her purse off a hook in the hallway. "We don't believe in the big allowances some of you kids get nowadays," she explained nervously to Willie, "so Spencer's may not seem like much to you. Anyway, Spencer, here's $10." Then, "But don't tell your father."

Willie noted that Spencer's wide eyes got even wider and more innocent. "Gee, Ma, you're a peach," he said on his way out the door.

"Bye, dear," she called after him.

"See?" he whispered right away to Willie. "Easy. If I'd turned the screws, I could've gotten a twenty. And my dad suckers for it, too, but I'm not supposed to tell my mom!"

"Is your allowance really only 50 cents?" Willie asked.

"Wouldn't have it any other way. I couldn't afford a bigger allowance. If it was bigger, I couldn't blackmail my folks any time I want like that, could I? Ya learnin' anything here, Willie?"

"Sure. Okay."

"Riiiight," they said together.

•

They had been downtown only five minutes when they ran into six of the other Top Dogs, all coming out of an arcade.

"Spence, where have you been?" said the tall girl with the makeup.

"With my buddy, ah, Willie here," he said, waving vaguely at Willie.

He introduced me as a buddy, Willie thought. *Does that make me a Top Dog? Be careful, don't seem too eager, and act cool with Miss Makeup or they won't like you,* he said to himself.

"Sandi," Spencer said to Miss Makeup, "ask my new friend if he'll spring for some sodas in those machines over there."

Sandi sidled up to Willie, leaned over, and said in a low voice in his ear, "Buy us some sodas, will you?" A shiver ran through Willie's body.

"Uh, all I have is a ten," Willie managed to say.

"Ten dollars? That'll do," she replied.

He pulled out the ten and gave it to her. She handed it to a boy with a weird haircut who was already moving toward the drug store.

When he came out he had a bag full of candy. Everybody helped themselves. "Had to get some change," he explained.

Then they all hit the pop machines with an avalanche of quarters. When it was all over, the boy

with the haircut said, "Here's your change, kid."
He gave Willie a nickel and two pennies.

Spencer came over and leaned on Willie like he
had done at Willie's observation post earlier in the
day. "See ya later, uh, kid," Spencer said to Willie.

Willie didn't know what to do.

"That ten dollars was my fee for teachin' ya a few
things," Spencer said.

"A few things?" Willie finally said.

Spencer had his wise guy look on for Willie.
"Yeah, that's all I got time for," Spencer said.

"I didn't learn a few things," Willie said.

"Oh?"

"No, I learned just one thing from you. Use people. That's it. That's your secret. You use people.
And the only reason you have any friends at all is
because these other 'dogs' are willing to run in a pack
and be used by you as long as they can be around
you. I don't know why they stick around. I thought
you were really something when I watched you from
a distance, but getting to know you—"

"Watch it, kid," Spencer said, leaning his full
weight on Willie, making him drop to his knees.

Then Spencer recovered his wide-eyed, innocent-
puppy look, motioned to the girls, and sauntered
off, leaving Willie on the ground.

"He does that look just to get you girls, you
know," Willie called out.

"We know," Miss Makeup said over her shoulder.
"It's cute."

Spencer turned around, looking very aloof, and said, "We're tired of this snoop now, aren't we, Top Dogs?"

"Sure. Okay. Riiiight," they all said together.

Willie's prayer: Boy, God, did I blow it by wanting to be like Spencer. Those people were really shallow. I went back to my notes and read them again before I threw them away. Everything seemed so dumb now that I know what Spencer's really like. Help him to realize that you can't go around using people like that. And help me to find friends who aren't so selfish. Amen.

Action idea: Sit near a place where there are a lot of people (like a playground, mall, airport, downtown, etc.). Take notes on what you see the people doing. Which people seem to be doing good and positive things? Which people seem to be doing negative or shallow things? If you value the people doing the good and positive things now, chances are you will become more and more like them as each year goes by.

"Be still, and know that I am God"
—Psalm 46:10

•

"Be still, boy. That's a she lion, and you can bet mountain lions have cubs this time of the year."
—*Old Fisherman*

Me, Myself, and God

Joe Casey was a rural Colorado boy to the hilt. He was a hiker, fisherman, camper, hunter, and biker—dirt bike, that is.

He had been a BMX biker since he was six, but last Christmas his mom and dad had chipped in to help him buy a used Suzuki RM250 motorcycle. It had been used pretty heavily for racing, but it was rugged and it worked.

"Don't go anywhere when we don't know about it," his mother always said as he was heading off into the countryside.

"Don't go tearing up the hills out there; stick to marked trails so nature doesn't kick you in the butt," his father would add.

One Saturday, Joe's parents were in town and Joe knew they would remain there all day. Joe had an itch to take the bike up a certain four-wheel drive trail on the other side of the valley. Joe figured the lake at the end of the trail was a good place to go to be alone. His dad had driven the family there once before for a picnic and Joe knew he'd come back alone some day.

He had brought up the subject twice with his dad but had only heard so far, "You don't want to do that. There's still snow on those trails up there. Besides, that's a trail with bigger boulders than you're used to. Takes a bigger vehicle to make it all the way to the lake."

Well, he didn't exactly say I couldn't go, did he? Joe mused. *He just said it would be tough. I'll do it!*

To get around his mother's warning not to go when she didn't know about it, he wrote a note indicating which trail he would be on—in case of an emergency—and left it on the kitchen table where she'd be sure to see it.

In spite of his having it all worked out why it was all right to go on this venture, Joe still was sure he'd have some explaining to do when he got home.

I don't care; it'll be worth a little explaining, he assured himself.

Joe packed a lunch in his backpack and, because of the dryness of the air in the mountains, brought plenty to drink. Then he put on his gloves and helmet, revved up the smooth motor, and took a moment to look up at the mountains.

Awesome. I'm lucky to have these to play on in my front yard, he thought. *Thank you, God.* Then he was off.

Joe's dad had called the sheriff once to see what he thought about Joe using a motorcycle that was built for off-road use—without a speedometer—on the county's backroads. "As long as he's careful out there, it's not illegal," the sheriff had said.

Joe passed the ranches of the valley and edged his way up the base of 11,000 foot Blanca Peak in the Sangre de Cristo mountain range.

Sangre de Cristo, the Blood of Christ; funny that something this beautiful and this peaceful would have such a gory name.

The lower part of the trail was a bit challenging to Joe, who wasn't entirely at home yet with the clutch in his left hand and the accelerator in his right. With a BMX bicycle he only had a brake in the right hand.

But Joe wove his way around the set boulders and loose granite and soon was feeling the rhythm of not trying to go too fast.

Coming around a bend in the trail that was more or less level, he allowed himself a moment to look at the spectacular aspens and rock formations. He splashed into the stream before he knew it, and tried to slow down so the spray wouldn't kill the engine. The rocks were harder to judge under the rushing water and Joe had to kick his foot down twice to catch his balance before reaching the other side.

Exhilarated, he hugged the dirt bike with his knees and felt the beauty of the mountain in the shaking of his body.

Joe met an elderly couple in a motorcycle with a sidecar coming down the trail. They stopped and talked.

"You can't get past the snow drifts up there, so I hope you're not planning to get to the lake today," the lady said.

"It's a great day for a jaunt anyway, don't you think?" the man suggested.

Joe wasn't much for small talk, so a minute later he was gone. Almost an hour later he was approaching the snowbanks.

The air was thin and crisp and he was feeling sharper in his maneuvering reflexes. He could see where the older couple had turned around, as well as two four-wheel drive vehicles sometime earlier. But those vehicles were all so wide, and Joe thought he saw enough room on the right to make a risky pass where the edge of the snow met a 10-foot embankment leading down to another stream. There was a single set of footprints there heading up the mountain but not down again. Whose?

He tried it—slowly—knowing full well that his dad would have had him turn around then and there. Then he passed left of the bank up ahead, skirting the trees, and amazingly he found that his way was mostly clear to the signs at the end of the trail.

Joe realized with a start that he was the first person to make it all the way up the trail this year! On a vehicle, anyway.

He switched off the engine, kicked the stand on the dirt bike, and took off his helmet. Then he chose the path marked Lower Trail to Lake and walked just one hundred yards before he began to break clear of the trees. The lake spread out before him.

And there, sitting on a log on the point that jutted out into the water, to Joe's surprise, sat a man with his back to Joe.

Joe called out, "Hello!" but the man didn't look up from his fishing, even though he was less than fifty paces away.

So Joe walked slowly out onto the point until he was almost to the man, who chose that moment to say, "It was just me, myself, and God up here until you came."

Then the silver-haired man—who looked strangely at home among the snow-capped peaks that surrounded them—turned his head and said, "Figures. A kid. You kids don't have enough room for all your noise down in the valley, so you have to ship it up here, I suppose."

This wasn't what it was supposed to be like up here, Joe thought. *I wanted to be alone. If I wanted to be chewed out, I could have gotten that anywhere.*

"I'll go somewhere else," Joe told the man, and he turned to go.

"Why are you here, boy? Someone call a taxi?"

"Look," Joe said, turning sharply back toward the man, "I'm here for the same reason you are. To be by myself."

The man looked at him closely, ignoring the red and white bobber that was signaling a catch. "Oh, it's never by yourself up here, you know. It's always me, myself, and God. And God is Creator, Redeemer, and Sanctifier, the three-in-one. At any given time, there are at least four of you up here even when you're alone—so to speak."

"I see."

"Sorry I got on your case, son. It's just that I've been hearing you coming up that trail for almost an hour. Some people say that there shouldn't be any motorized vehicles on the mountain at all. You oughta walk next time. Takes longer, but you see more than just boulders."

At that moment, Joe saw a brown shadow pass among some trees a stone's throw to his left. Joe assumed the man had brought a dog.

"Well," Joe replied, "I guess I'll leave you alone—so to speak. I'm out of here." Then he turned without further comment and retraced his path to his dirt bike.

A minute later, just before he started the motorcycle, the old man called, "Boy! Boy!"

Joe could no longer see the man because of the trees, but he grudgingly yelled, "Yeah?"

"Come here, let me see your cycle. Drive it down here. Quickly!"

Part of Joe didn't want to go back to the lake, but the man sounded like it was important.

He started up the bike, adjusted his helmet, and steered toward the lake. As he came up behind the man, the old fisherman was calmly stowing his gear in his tackle box. His fish were flopping in the pebbles on the shore. The man pointed and looked to the right. Joe followed his gaze.

A tan-colored animal had emerged from the woods fifty yards around the shoreline. *The man's dog,* Joe thought. *So what?* Then the animal *pounced* further up the side of the mountain, turned, and glowered at the humans.

There's no dog that can move like that. A mountain lion! Joe realized.

Joe sucked in a quick breath.

"Be still, boy. That's a she lion, and you can bet mountain lions have cubs this time of year."

"Ahh, but—"

"If we leave the fish flopping here, maybe she'll be interested in them."

Joe revved his engine. The big cat flinched.

"So," the man said nonchalantly, "you got a gun?"

Joe shook his head.

"Neither have I."

They watched the lion move with wary grace, danger signaled in each step as she watched the two intruders.

"Well, I believe I'm the one who called for the taxi," the silver-haired man said kindly. "Normally, I don't like noise up here, but do you suppose you could make that motorcycle of yours sound like a *bigger* mountain lion and get us down this mountain?"

"I suppose so," Joe replied.

"It's getting crowded up here anyway," the old man said, "what with Father, Son, and Holy Spirit, and you and me and a big cat."

The man climbed onto the back of the motorcycle. Joe revved the engine again. The cat slowly backed away. "What do you say we ease on down the trail and give some solitude to our new friend?"

"You bet!" Joe said.

As the sound of the motor's roar trailed down the mountain, two mountain lion kittens joined their mother, and she licked them lovingly.

Joe's prayer: On the way down the mountain, that fisherman taught me about that word, solitude. *When God isn't with you and you're by yourself, it's loneliness. But with God there with you, it's solitude. I like that word. Thank you for giving me some solitude at the lake today, even if it was for such a short while. Let's do it again soon. Amen.*

Action idea: Next time you feel like getting away by yourself, remember that with God with you, you don't ever have to be lonely.